IRAN DOUBLES DOWN ON TERROR AND TURMOIL

First published in 2018 by
National Council of Resistance of Iran – U.S. Representative Office (NCRI-US), 1747 Pennsylvania Ave., NW, Suite 1125, Washington, DC 20006

ISBN-10 (paperback): 1-944942-23-8
ISBN-13 (paperback): 978-1-944942-23-6

ISBN-10 (e-book): 1-944942-24-6
ISBN-13 (e-book): 978-1-944942-24-3

Library of Congress Control Number: 2018913038
Library of Congress Cataloging-in-Publication Data

National Council of Resistance of Iran – U.S. Representative Office.

Iran Doubles Down on Terror and Turmoil

1. Iran. 2. Ballistic Missiles. 3. Terrorism. 4. Nuclear. 5. Middle East

First Edition: November 2018

Printed in the United States of America

These materials are being distributed by the National Council of Resistance of Iran-U.S. Representative Office. Additional information is on file with the Department of Justice, Washington, D.C.

Table of Contents

Executive Summary

After nearly forty years of religious dictatorship, Iran observers both inside and abroad now concede that the regime is facing unprecedented existential threats. 2018 began with the Iranian people rising up in more than 140 cities and towns, demanding the ouster of the *velayat-e faqih* (absolute clerical rule). The popular uprising against the regime has been both deepening and spreading in the ensuing months.

Mismanagement and plunder has left the country's economy in shambles, supplying a major cause for sustained public grievances. The value of the national currency has lost 70% of its value in 2018, unemployment and inflation are rampant, and two thirds of the populace is living below the poverty line, among other major indicators. Meanwhile, the regime's isolation continues to grow regionally and internationally, a trend that is expected to continue with further sanctions and censures.

Against this backdrop, the regime lacks the necessary ideological and political capital to resolve such foundational predicaments. As threats close in, the regime in its desperation has opted to step up terrorism and warmongering. This is not only an Iranian problem, it is a major international concern as the regime's elaborate regional designs coalesce with its growing appetite for terrorism as a means for survival.

This report examines the motivation behind the regime's political and economic strategy by considering three areas: terrorism, incitement of regional conflicts, and the ballistic missile threat.

Chapter one offers a synopsis of Tehran's latest terrorist schemes and attacks. Failing to quell growing popular protests against their rule, the mullahs have opted to bolster domestic suppression with blatant terrorism and intimidation, particularly against opponents. This new strategy targets the most viable political alternative, the National Council of Resistance of Iran (NCRI), and its leading member, the People's Mojahedin Organization of Iran (PMOI/MEK). The strategy revolves around terrorism and physical annihilation of opponents. It is perceived to be so vital to the regime's longevity that its officials are willing to risk serious international diplomatic backlash and resources in Europe in a bid to deal a devastating blow to the organized opposition. For the first time in its history, a regime diplomat in Tehran's embassy in Austria has been caught red-handed directing a bombing operation on European soil. German authorities have officially accused the so-called diplomat with personally providing a bomb intended for detonation at a major opposition rally in Paris on June 30, 2018. The August 2018 foiled plot in the United States is another indication that the regime is willing to take high risks even within the United States to deliver blows to the members of the main Iranian opposition movement which has been very effective in undermining the regime inside Iran as well as exposing it abroad.

Chapter two reviews Tehran's much more pronounced orientation toward policies of warmongering and meddling in Syria, Yemen, Iraq, and Lebanon, including terrorist training camps run by the Qods Force, the extraterritorial arm of the Islamic Revolutionary Guard Corps (IRGC). The mullahs' regime has funneled billions of dollars to finance its belligerent war agenda in the Middle East while the majority of Iran's people are living in poverty. As the regime's officials have conceded, if the regime fails to inflame wars outside Iran's borders, it would have to fight for survival within Iran's borders. This is because external conflicts draw attention away from domestic crises.

Chapter three reviews the regime's ballistic missile strategy. Tehran is setting up the necessary facilities and equipment for missiles development and launch capabilities. Moreover, it does not just fire missiles into regional countries in pursuit of war; it also exports the necessary missile technology and constructs missile factories outside Iran's borders. This export of missiles to Yemen and elsewhere contravenes UN Security Council resolutions.

The final chapter offers viable solutions that can frustrate and thwart Tehran's terrorism designs and warmongering. It concludes with the urgent need for the UN Security Council to adopt a decisive policy vis-à-vis the regime. The Iranian people seek precisely such international support in their quest for a free, democratic, and secular republic in Iran.

Introduction

Today, after forty years of rule, the Iranian regime is encircled by domestic and international crises. These political, economic, social, regional and international crises have emerged from four decades of suppression in Iran and terrorism and warmongering abroad. The regime is on the brink of collapse, with no solution in sight other than changing the government. The regime's Supreme Leader, Ali Khamenei, joined by its President, Hassan Rouhani, is trying to delay the dictatorship's overthrow by intensifying the suppression of the people's uprising, stepping up terrorism and increasing warmongering, including hollow shows of force and aggravating crises like the war in Syria.

For example, in a speech at Noshahr Naval Academy on September 8, 2018, Supreme Leader Khamenei asked the armed forces to increase Iran's military strength, declaring that U.S. "plots" in Syria, Iraq and Lebanon "have failed," implicitly underscoring the regime's intervention in these countries. [1]

Hossein Dehqan, a Khamenei advisor in military affairs and Minister of Defence in Rouhani's first cabinet, explicitly highlighted the persistence of the regime's involvement in Syria, saying in an interview with Russia Today on September 7, 2018: "If the Syrian government and the Syrian people want to confront the U.S. on the

---

1 Khamenei's official website, September 8, 2018.

eastern Euphrates and if they request help from Iran, Iran stands ready to provide military support to Syria on this front."[2]

The regime's President, Hassan Rouhani, has also expressed support on multiple occasions for the Islamic Revolutionary Guard Corps (IRGC), their involvement in the region and missile attacks. On May 22, 2017, for example, following Tehran's presidential elections, Rouhani said: "Those who have been able to stand up to terrorists have been the nation of Iraq, the nation of Syria and the nation of Lebanon. And through its diplomats and military advisors, the nation of Iran has helped and will help these two great nations and other peoples."[3]

---

2   Fars News Agency, September 7, 2018.
3   Fars News Agency, May 22, 2017.

Chapter 1:
Terrorism against the Alternative, the Regime's Only Answer to the Iranian People's Uprising

In late 2017 and early 2018, the clerical regime faced a situation, which impacted its entire equilibrium. Nationwide protests by the Iranian people erupted with the intention of overthrowing the regime. In over 140 cities, the Iranian people rose up against the regime and demanded overthrow, shaking the clerical regime to its core. The continuation of these anti-regime protests in the first eight months of 2018 has been the main feature of Iranian politics. On August 28, 2018, in a speech at the Majlis (parliament), Rouhani acknowledged that the protests had triggered a crisis for the regime: "All of a sudden, the country's climate changed. ... The slogans gradually ... turned into structure-shattering slogans. ... Such an incident was rare in all the previous years."

Since the outset of the protests, some of the regime's highest ranking officials pointed to the People's Mojahedin Organization of Iran (MEK/MEK) as the party responsible for organizing the uprisings, vowing a firm response. The Secretary of the Supreme National

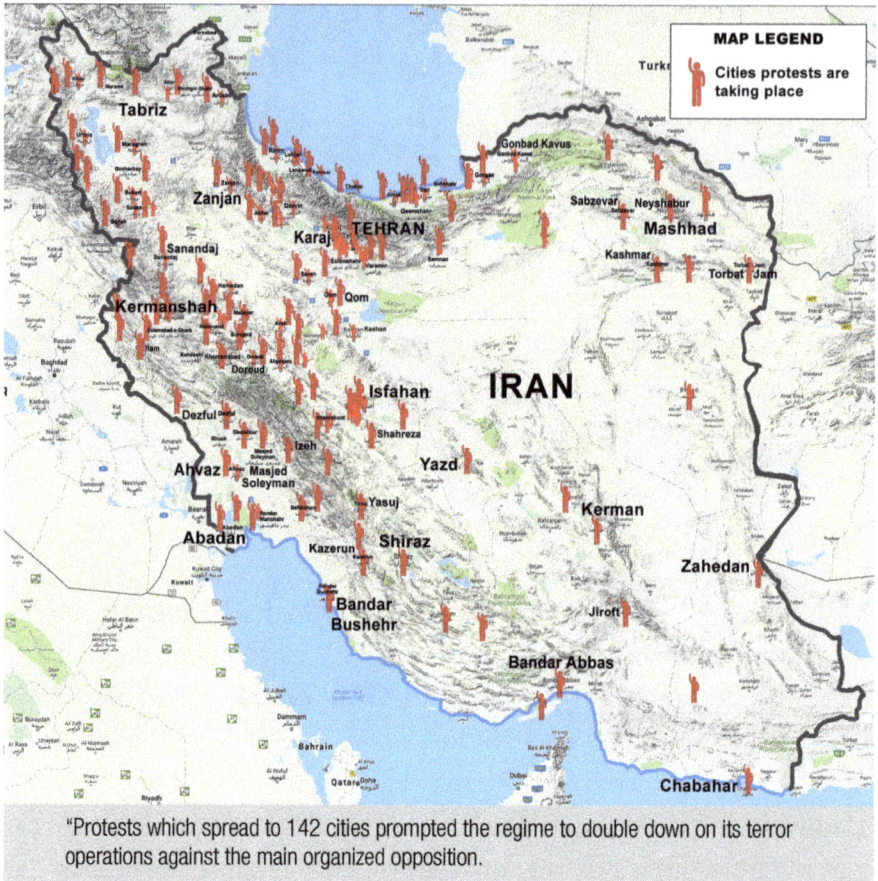

"Protests which spread to 142 cities prompted the regime to double down on its terror operations against the main organized opposition.

Security Council, Ali Shamkhani, said on the fifth day of the mass uprising (January 1, 2018): "The goal of organized foreign intervention is to prevent progress in Iran, and therefore, they are trying to bring about the collapse of the country from within." Shamkhani added that the MEK "will get the appropriate answer from a source they do not know."

On January 2, 2018, Rouhani had an hour-long phone conversation with the French President, urging Emmanuel Macron to adopt practical measures against the MEK in France.

On January 9, 2018, Khamenei stressed that the uprising was organized by the MEK and that they had planned for it for months. He threatened that "this effort will not remain without consequences," adding: "There has to be a raising of awareness and conversations vis-a-vis people who entered the scene out of excitement, whether they were university students or not. However, the case of the MEK is different."

Since January 2018, the clerical regime has exhibited little or no solutions to address the Iranian people's needs. It views the answer only in its attempts to harm the organized opposition and alternative, particularly through acts of terrorism. In its cost-benefit analysis, and in view of the urgency and gravity of the situation, it has deemed that any diplomatic price or consequence resulting from such measures would be acceptable.

Terrorist plot targeting the MEK in Albania

In the aftermath of rocket attacks and the massacre of MEK members at the hands of Iranian regime agents in Iraq in May 2013, and soon after the government of Albania began accepting them that same year, the regime's Ministry of Intelligence and Security (MOIS) sent its intelligence agents to its embassy in Tirana. Albania is a very small country, and the Iranian embassy never had more than two or three diplomats, whether during the era of the shah or the rule of the clerics. But since the MEK members have taken up residence there, the mullahs' embassy in Albania has become one of the most important Iranian embassies in Europe.

MOIS agent Fereydoun Zandi Ali Abadi set up the first intelligence station in Tirana. He was the head of station from early 2014 to 2017, and his primary mission was gathering intelligence on the MEK and identifying their whereabouts in Albania.[4]

In 2016, MOIS Deputy for International Affairs Gholamhossein Mohammadnia became the regime's ambassador in Albania[5], and the embassy increasingly came under the control of MOIS agents.

In 2017 Mostafa Roudaki,[6] who had been in charge of the intelligence station in the regime's embassy in Austria, became the head of station in Albania, and was tasked with increasing the espionage and terrorist activities against the MEK.

A terror plot against the MEK planned by the MOIS and the regime's intelligence station in Albania on the eve of the Iranian New Year celebration (Nowruz) in March 2018 was foiled by the security services of Albania.[7]

In an interview with Vision Plus TV on April 19, 2018, Prime Minister Eddie Rama referred to the threat posed by the regime's terrorist attacks, saying the Albanian

---

4   Statement of Security and Counter- terrorism Committee of the National Council of Resistance of Iran, December 3, 2014

5   ibid, February 5, 2018

6   Opcit

7   Iran plots terror on European soil as EU tries to shield regime from Trump sanctions push, Fox News, August 9, 2018, Adam Shaw, http://www.foxnews.com/politics/2018/08/09/iran-plots-terror-on-european-soil-as-eu-tries-to-shield-regime-from-trump-sanctions-push.html

The Iranian regime embassy in Tirana, Albania is where terror plotes are planned

government along with other European countries was taking action against terrorist plots.[8]

On July 5, 2018, the US Department of State announced that two Iranian agents had been arrested on terrorism charges by Albanian authorities on March 22, 2018.[9]

According to Belgian police officials, the Albanian police and intelligence services were among the countries involved in the joint operation to arrest Asadullah Assadi and foil the terrorist plot against the Iranian opposition gathering in Paris.[10]

---

8   Interview of Edi Rama, Prime Minister of Albania, Vizion Plus Tv, April 19, 2018.

9   Iran: Select Europe-Based Operational Activity, 1979-2018, Fact sheet of the US Department of State on the Iranian terrorism in Europe, complied by the National Counterterrorsim Center, July 5, 2018, https://www.state.gov/j/ct/rls/other/283789.htm.

10 "Iran Plotted To Bomb A Meeting Near Paris That Former US Officials Attended, Germany Says," Buzzfeed News, July 11, 2018, Mitch Prothero, https://www.buzzfeednews.com/article/mitchprothero/germany-has-charged-an-iranian-diplomat-with-plotting-to

IRAN: SELECT EUROPE-BASED OPERATIONAL ACTIVITY, 1979-2018

Attack
Includes assassinations, bombings, cyberattacks, kidnappings and hostage-taking, hijackings, and small-arms attacks

Attack planning disrupted
Includes the detainment and arrest of operatives, discovery of weapons and explosives caches, and detection of surveillance

State-supported attack
Includes attacks by nonstate actors with direct financial or logistical support or lethal aid from Iran

Support to state and nonstate actors
Includes ongoing support to Syria or select instances of support to militant or terrorist groups

DATE	LOCATION	ACTIVITY/EVENT
22 MAR 2018	Tirana, Albania	Two Iranian operatives were arrested on charges of terrorism by Albanian authorities
2016-2018	Germany	German authorities searched the homes and offices of 10 suspected IRGC-QF operatives in early 2018; in 2016 German authorities arrested an IRGC-QF operative for spying on the ex-head of a German-Israeli group and people close to him
APR 2013	Bosnia and Herzegovina	Two Iranian diplomats were discovered to be Iranian intelligence officers and were expelled for espionage and connections to terrorism
2012	Turkey	Four IRGC-QF operatives entered Turkey to attack Israeli targets; the attack was disrupted by Turkish authorities
JUL 2012	Sofia, Bulgaria	An IRGC-QF operative was arrested by Bulgarian authorities for surveilling a synagogue
20 FEB 1996	Istanbul, Turkey	Iranian operatives murdered a member of the National Council for Resistance of Iran
17 SEP 1992	Berlin, Germany	Lebanese Hizballah assassinated four Iranian Kurdish dissidents in a small-arms attack at a café; Iran provided logistical support; four operatives were tried and convicted in 1997
6 AUG 1991	Suresnes, France	Iranian operatives assassinated the former Iranian Prime Minister Shahpour Bakhtiar who led an anti-Iranian regime movement; one operative was convicted, two fled
13 JUL 1989	Vienna, Austria	Iranian operatives using diplomatic cover assassinated the head of an Iranian Kurdish dissident group and two others
DEC 1985-SEP 1986	Paris, France	Lebanese Hizballah bombed a number of soft targets; Iran provided logistical support; 12 were killed, at least 200 wounded

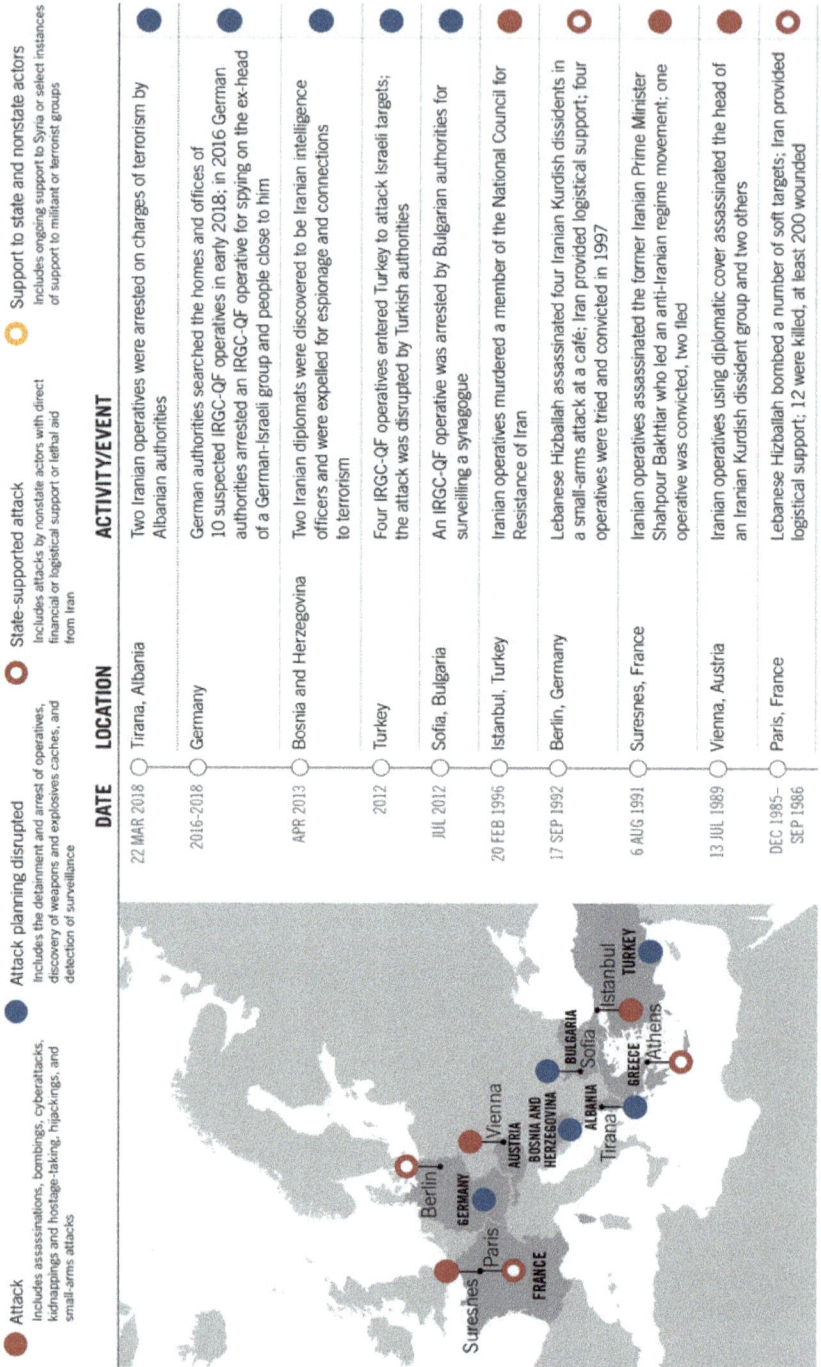

State Department lists the plot by the Iranian regime against the MEK location in Tirana as part of its select terror activities of the regime in Europe.

Terrorist plot against the opposition rally in Paris

On June 30, 2018, another terrorist operation with the objective of bombing the large gathering of the Iranian Resistance in Villepinte (suburbs of Paris) was neutralized hours before the planned explosion. Tens of thousands of people were joined at the Paris rally by nearly 600 political dignitaries from close to 70 countries around the world, including the U.S., Europe and the Middle East.

Two regime agents, Amir Saadouni and Nasimeh Naami, were arrested carrying the explosives. A regime diplomat based in Austria, Assadollah Assadi, was the

Iranian Resistance grand gathering in Paris on June 30, 2018 was the target of Tehran's foiled terror plot

mastermind. According to German federal prosecutors, the diplomat had personally handed the bomb to the terrorists in Luxembourg. He was subsequently arrested in Germany on July 1. An additional person named Mehrdad Arefani was arrested in France in this regard and extradited to Belgium.

Germany extradited Assadi to Belgium on October 10th, to stand trial with other culprits who are all in prison, awaiting judicial processes in Brussels. On October 26, 2018, Reuters reported that France had expelled an Iranian diplomat based in Paris, for his involvement in the June 30th terror plot. Sources said the diplomat was an Iranian intelligence operative under diplomatic cover. France also froze assets belonging to Tehran's intelligence services and two senior Iranian officials.

In a rare joint statement, the French interior, foreign and economy ministers said: "This extremely serious act envisaged on our territory could not go without a response.

"In taking this decision, France underlines its determination to fight against terrorism in all its forms, particularly on its own territory."

The plan demonstrated that Tehran has no qualms about conducting a terrorist attack leading to the possible deaths of very high-profile American and European personalities, or about the scale of European and American casualties.

The Organization for Foreign Intelligence and Movements

The MOIS office responsible for conducting extraterritorial terrorist operations, particularly on European and American territories, is called the Organization for Foreign Intelligence and Movements (OFIM). MOIS stations abroad, and specifically those at the regime's embassies are tied to OFIM.

The head of OFIM in the MOIS is Reza Amiri Moqaddam. He is considered one of the highest security officials of the Iranian regime and reports to the Minister of Intelligence, currently Mahmoud Alavi. He is the key figure for the regime's terrorist operations outside Iran, particularly in Europe and the U.S.

Amiri Moqaddam was an IRGC member during the Iran-Iraq War in the 1980s. He later transferred over to

REZA AMIRI MOGHADDAM
HEAD OF THE MOIS FOREIGN INTELLIGENCE
AND MOVEMENTS ORGANIZATION

Reza Amiri Moghaddam attends a
meeting with the US delegation in Iraq

Reza Amiri Moqaddam heads OFIM of the Ministry of Intelligence

MOIS. He was the deputy for the Directorate of Foreign Intelligence and Movements prior to the re-organization of this entity, when it was elevated to the Organization for Foreign Intelligence and Movements.

During the years when American forces established a presence in Iraq, Amiri Moqaddam was specifically focused on Iraq and operations against Coalition Forces there. During the tripartite negotiations in Iraq between Iraq, the U.S., and the Iranian regime in 2007 and 2008, Amiri Moqaddam was one of the key figures in the regime's delegation. He negotiated with Ryan Crocker, then-U.S. ambassador to Iraq, under the guise of the diplomatic delegation.

Assadollah Assadi, the regime's station chief in Austria and coordinator of MOIS stations in Europe

Assadollah Assadi is the Iranian regime's MOIS station chief in Vienna, Austria. Since 2014, he has been responsible for coordinating Tehran's intelligence stations across Europe. In view of the sensitivity and significance of the planned Paris bombing against the main opposition, the command of this terrorist operation was assigned to Assadi.

Vienna has been the coordination center for MOIS stations in Europe for several years. Since 2014, Assadi has been on assignment as the third secretary of the regime's embassy, working from the third floor of the

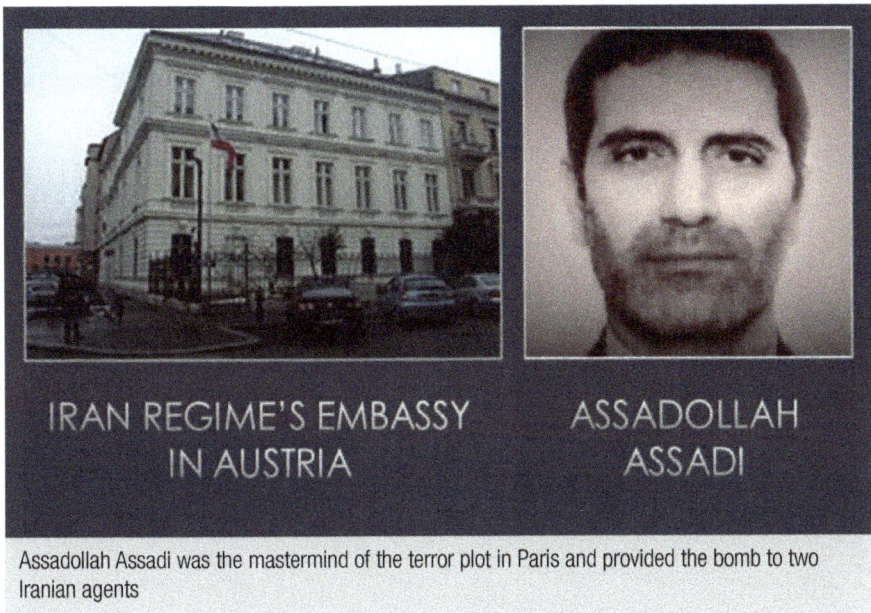

IRAN REGIME'S EMBASSY
IN AUSTRIA

ASSADOLLAH
ASSADI

Assadollah Assadi was the mastermind of the terror plot in Paris and provided the bomb to two Iranian agents

Vienna embassy, holding the key MOIS position in Europe, and reporting directly to Reza Amiri Moqaddam, the head of OFIM.

Assadi is a senior MOIS officer, involved in plotting terrorist operations with special expertise in destruction and bombings. He has had significant training in this regard. He has also had training in intelligence-gathering and surveillance.

Assadi was born in Khorramabad in the western province of Lorestan in 1971. He entered the MOIS following the Iran-Iraq War, starting in the provincial intelligence office in Khorramabad. One of his focus areas in MOIS at that time was the arrest and suppression of the MEK and other dissidents. He was later promoted and became involved in operations planning, specifically terrorist operations.

Assadi's record is quite telling. Following the U.S. invasion of Iraq in 2003, Assadi was appointed third consul in the Iranian embassy in Baghdad in early 2004. He retained this position until mid-2008, after which he was replaced by an MOIS officer named Kiomars Reshadatmand (aka Haj Ali). A document in our possession shows the Iranian regime's Ministry of Foreign Affairs requesting a visa for Reshadatmand as a replacement for Assadi, confirming that Assadi was in Iraq until 2008 — the height of the bombings and killings in that country. Assadi played a decisive role in terrorist plots, bombings and kidnappings in Iraq against Coalition Forces, the MEK, and Iraqi citizens from 2004 to 2008.

Plotting terrorist operations in the U.S.

On August 9, 2018, two Iranians, Ahmadreza Mohammadi-Doostdar, 38, and Majid Ghorbani, 59, were arrested by the FBI in the U.S. The U.S. Department of Justice, District of Columbia, issued the indictment for these arrests on August 20, 2018. The indictment alleges that the two Iranian citizens and residents of California were conducting covert surveillance of Israeli and Jewish facilities in the United States, as well as collecting information about American citizens and other U.S. nationals who are members of the MEK.[11]

---

11 Two Individuals Charged For Acting as Illegal Agents of the Government of Iran, Release by the Department of Justice, August 20, 2018, https://www.justice.gov/usao-dc/pr/two-individuals-charged-acting-illegal-agents-government-iran

The charges were announced by Assistant Attorney General for National Security John Demers, U.S. Attorney Jessie K. Liu for the District of Columbia, and Acting Executive Assistant Director Michael McGarrity of the FBI's National Security Branch.

"Doostdar and Ghorbani are alleged to have acted on behalf of Iran, including by conducting surveillance of political opponents and engaging in other activities that could put Americans at risk," said Assistant Attorney General Demers.

Acting Executive Assistant Director McGarrity added: "This alleged activity demonstrates a continued interest in targeting the United States, as well as potential opposition groups located in the United States."

According to the indictment, "in or about July 2017, Doostdar traveled to the United States from Iran in order to collect intelligence information about entities and individuals considered by the government of Iran to be enemies of that regime, including Israeli and Jewish interests, and individuals associated with the MEK, a group that advocates the overthrow of the current Iranian government."

On or about July 21, 2017, Doostdar is alleged to have conducted surveillance of the Rohr Chabad House, a Jewish institution located in Chicago, including photographing the security features surrounding the facility, according to the Department of Justice.

According to the signed criminal complaint and affidavit, "A human target package includes information collected about an individual, such as the official position of the individual; an analysis of personal vulnerabilities or other opportunities to exploit the individual; and confirmation of the identity and location of the individual. Finally, a target package could enable a neutralization plan, which may include apprehension, recruitment, cyber exploitation, or capture/kill operations."[12]

Court-authorized electronic surveillance revealed Ghorbani telling Doostdar that "he saw the individual who 'leaked the nuclear program'... Jafarzadeh, who is the head of the NCR here — with Safavi..."

The Associated Press reported, "Court document indicate that one of the people targeted was Alireza Jafarzadeh, deputy director of National Council of Resistance of Iran-Washington office. His revelations about Iran's nuclear sites in 2002 triggered the first inspections in Iran by the International Atomic Energy Agency."[13]

Ghorbani also mentions that he saw Ali Safavi, another official of the NCRI during a rally in New York, adding that another participant in the rally "needs one-one shot," apparently referring to a gun shot.

According to reports obtained from inside the regime, the case of the two MOIS agents in the U.S. has been turned over to the MOIS in Iran. The MOIS is following it with the assistance of the Iranian regime's Foreign Ministry.

---

12 United States of America vs. Majig Ghorbani and Ahmadreza Mohammadi-Doostdar, signed criminal complaint, August 8, 2018 available on the Department of Justice website, https://www.justice.gov/ usao-dc/press-release/file/1088526/download and https://www.justice.gov/ usao-dc/press-release/file/1088531/download

13 Riechmann, Deb, "2 alleged agents of Iran arrested for spying in US," The Associated Press, August 25, 2018, https://www.apnews.com/ ec9c2b547c5043938d1bdba4a4f724b9

Copies of all reports produced in the Foreign Ministry regarding the case are submitted to the MOIS office at the Foreign Ministry, which is called the "Office for Evaluating Reports." A dossier has been opened for the two detained individuals, containing all of the compiled reports, including the account of the arrests, reports on the indictments, and a letter regarding the identities of the two individuals.

In 2017 and 2018, the regime's terrorist activities in Iraq against Iranian dissidents, especially Kurdish activists, were stepped up. These attacks occurred on July 14, 2017, and on March 6, March 30, April 12, and July 18, 2018. The most deadly attack took place on September 8, 2018.

Upsurge in regime's terrorist operations in past two years (Europe and U.S.)

Also in the Middle East, there was an upsurge of terror operations against the dissidents. In 2017 and 2018, the clerical regime's terrorist activities significantly increased. Nine instances have been outlined in the table below. As shown, the activities took place in the U.S., France, Germany, Belgium, the UK, the Netherlands, and Turkey. It also explains the extensive scope of the regime's terrorist operations in Western countries. In recent years and following the signing of the nuclear deal (Joint Comprehensive Plan of Action, JCPOA), the clerical regime exploited the West's appeasement policy to expand its terrorist operations in these territories. Also in the Middle East, there was an upsurge of terror operations against the dissidents.

Date	Country	Description
Aug. 9, 2018	U.S.A.	Two Iranians, Ahmadreza Mohammadi-Doostdar, 38, and Majid Ghorbani, 59, were arrested by the FBI in the United States. They were gathering intelligence for the regime's Ministry of Intelligence and Security (MOIS).
June 30, 2018	France	The regime's MOIS set in motion a sophisticated terrorist plot involving its diplomat-terrorists, including Assadollah Assadi stationed in its embassy in Austria. Several other individuals were also involved. The plot aimed to detonate a car bomb at the MEK rally in Villepinte near Paris. The scheme was neutralized through the efforts of Belgian, German and French police. Those involved were arrested.
Mar. 22, 2018	Albania	The regime's MOIS plotted to set off a truck bomb near a hall where a Persian New Year celebration was being held. Two regime agents who had entered Albania under the guise of reporters were arrested and the conspiracy was neutralized.
Feb. 5, 2018	Turkey	Arash Shoja Shargh, a dissident journalist, disappeared in Van, a city in central Turkey.
Jan. 16, 2018	Germany	On the orders of the German Federal Prosecutor's Office, German special forces raided the homes and centers of 10 spies and agents tied to the IRGC's Quds Force residing in various German provinces, leading to their arrests. The investigations were conducted in the states of Berlin, Württemberg, Baden, Bayern, and North Rhine-Westphalia.
Jan. 16, 2018	Germany	Espionage targeting a former head of a German-Israeli association by a 10-person group of the regime's terrorists continued for two years until 2018. The plot was uncovered by German police.

Date	Country	Description
Jan. 11, 2018	Britain	A failed terrorist plot was conducted against Mahmoud Ahmad, an Ahvazi activist.
Nov. 8, 2017	The Nether- lands	Ahmad Mola Nissi, a leader of the al-Ahvazieh Movement, was shot dead in front of his house when an assailant armed with a gun and a silencer, got out of a Mercedes and shot Nissi in the back. The Dutch security office expelled two Iranian diplomats in June 2018 in connection with terrorist acts of the Iranian regime in the Netherlands.
Apr. 29, 2017	Turkey	Saeed Karimian, the head of the Jam TV channel, and another individual were shot dead by two masked gunmen who stopped Karimian's car. Turkish police subsequently arrested the assassin, an Iranian national who was a drug trafficking ringleader in Turkey.

The regime's decision-making and executive agencies for terrorist operations

All decisions on terrorist attacks abroad, particularly those targeting Iranian dissidents, are made at the highest levels of the Iranian regime. Such sensitive and sophisticated operations require high levels of intelligence, coordination, logistics, and operational skills, as well as the political and diplomatic cover terrorist operatives need.

Here are key decision-making and executive agencies involved for terrorist operations.

The Special Affairs Office of the Supreme Leader:
Following the death of the regime's former Supreme
Leader, Ruhollah Khomeini, Ali Khamenei appointed
mullah Ali-Asghar Mirhejazi, then-head of the foreign
office of the Foreign Ministry, to establish a special
intelligence and security apparatus called the "Special
Affairs Office" to operate out of Khamenei's office.
The Special Affairs Office coordinates the regime's
intelligence, security and terrorist organs within
Khamenei's office. All terrorist operations are conducted
under the supervision of the Special Affairs Office
after Khamenei's personal approval. Mullah Mirhejazi
was added to the list of EU sanctions in March 2012.
On May 30, 2013, his name was included in the list of
U.S. sanctions as the Security Deputy to the Supreme
Leader.[14]

Supreme National Security Council (SNSC): The
SNSC is the highest decision-maker in defence-security
affairs. It is chaired by the president, currently Hassan
Rouhani. Its standing members include the regime's
Judiciary Chief, Speaker of Parliament, the Head of
the Management and Planning Organization of Iran,
the SNSC Secretary, the Representative of the Supreme
Leader, the Second Representative of the Supreme
Leader, the Chief of Staff for the Armed Forces, the
IRGC Commander-in-Chief, the Commander-in-Chief
of the Army, the Foreign Minister, the Intelligence
minister, and the Interior Minister. Decisions regarding
the regime's terrorist operations are adopted in the
Supreme National Security Council.

---

14 https://www.treasury.gov/resource-center/sanctions/OFAC-Enforcement/
   Pages/20130530.aspx

Ministry of Intelligence and Security (MOIS):
The MOIS is the regime's most important institution in conducting terrorist operations abroad, especially in Western countries. The Foreign Affairs Committee of the National Council of Resistance of Iran (NCRI) published a comprehensive and detailed dossier in August 2018 regarding the role of MOIS stations in the regime's European embassies vis-a-vis terrorist operations, including the role of the MOIS itself in terrorism.

The Intelligence Coordination Council is established under the supervision of the Intelligence Minister in the Supreme National Security Council. This council is composed of the Intelligence Minister, the Foreign Minister, the Interior Minister, the Head of the IRGC's Intelligence Organization, the Head of the IRGC's Intelligence Protection Organization, the Army's Intelligence Deputy, the Head of the Army's Intelligence Protection Organization, the Commander of the State Security Forces (NAJA), the Head of NAJA's Intelligence Protection Organization, the Head of the Intelligence Protection Organization of the Defence Ministry, and the Head of the Intelligence Protection Organization of the Commander-in-Chief.

IRGC Quds Force: The IRGC formed the extraterritorial Quds Force to meddle in the affairs of other countries. The Quds Force is the IRGC's arm for terrorist operations and warmongering in other countries.

The IRGC Quds Force has conducted many terrorist operations, particularly after 2009, in various countries in North America, Europe, Asia and Africa. It has created a separate unit for terrorist operations called Unit 400.

This unit is responsible for the provision of military support, training and guidance of terrorist agents and guerilla organizations in various parts of the world. The Quds Force uses foreign agents in various countries in which it has influence, such as members of the Lebanese Hezbollah, to conduct its terrorist operations.

The IRGC Intelligence Organization: The IRGC's Intelligence Organization was created in June 2009, four months after the start of the 2009 uprisings, as a result of the amalgamation of IRGC intelligence and a number of other intelligence-related bodies in the IRGC. The head of the Organization is Hossein Taeb. The Organization has direct contacts with Khamenei's office. The IRGC's Intelligence Organization plays a role both in domestic suppression and in the regime's terrorist activities abroad. The Organization uses the Bassij Organization to gather intelligence and conduct surveillance against all sectors of Iranian society.

Chapter 2:
Expansion of Regional Warmongering and Meddling

Persistence of warmongering in Syria

Syria has been one of the most important targets for the Iranian regime and its IRGC. In the course of the Iran-Iraq War in the 1980s, former Syrian President Hafez al-Assad was among those who provided political and military support to the regime and the IRGC. When the Arab Spring blossomed in 2011, the people of Syria also began their protests against Bashar al-Assad's dictatorship, threatening his rule. In response, Khamenei dispatched the IRGC's forces to prop up Assad. Khamenei and other IRGC officials have stressed on multiple occasions that if the regime's forces fail in Syria, they will be forced to fight inside Iran, revealing the essential role that the Syrian strategy plays in preserving the clerical dictatorship.

Extent of the mullahs' interference in the Syrian Civil War, and the budget allotted for its Syrian agenda: The following brief summary is intended to clarify the extent of Tehran's meddling in the Syrian War, and the cost of that interference paid from the Iranian people's pocket:

The regime spends 15-20 billion dollars annually on the Syrian conflict. The sum total is estimated at more than 100 billion dollars.[15] The total number of foreign forces including the Islamic Revolutionary Guards Corps, Afghan Fatemiyoun, the Pakistani Zeynabiyoun, various Iraqi militia, the Lebanese Hezbollah, and various other groups taking part in the war under the IRGC totaled 70,000 in January 2016.[16] (The number of foreign fighters affiliated with the IRGC dropped after the siege of Aleppo in December 2016.)

The total number of forces under IRGC command in Syria, including foreign forces and Syrian mercenaries, exceeds 100,000.[17] The total number of casualties among IRGC affiliated forces (Iranian and non-Iranian) in Syria until January 2016 exceeded 10,000.[18] In the succeeding two years, casualty counts increased dramatically, and are ongoing. Approximately 100 senior IRGC commanders ranked higher than colonel have been killed.[19] One IRGC Commander named Zarib estimated that 25 – 30% of IRGC members in Syria had been killed or wounded. In other words, of every ten forces deployed to Syria by the mullahs' regime, three had been killed or wounded.[20]

----

15 *How Iran Fuels Syria War*, National Council of Resistance of Iran – U.S. Representative Office, November 2016

16 ibid

17 Statement of the Secretariat of the National Council of Resistance of Iran - 2017

18 *How Iran Fuels Syria War*, National Council of Resistance of Iran – U.S. Representative Office, November 2016

19 The specifics of approximately 60 IRGC commanders were gathered prior to November 2016 and are listed in *How Iran Fuels Syria War*.

20 Site Farhang News – IRGC Brigadier General Hamid Abazar, successor to the commander of the IRGC's Imam Khomeini University, January 2, 2016

The Formation of the IRGC's Invasion of Syria:
The IRGC has divided Syria into a number of military
fronts, assigning commanders and centers for its forces
in each of these regions. As the Syrian Army's ground
troops weaken, the IRGC and affiliated militias play
a definitive role as ground forces, as will be explained in
more detail below.

Command HQ: The IRGC's command center in Syria is
located in the province of Damascus. The Glass Building
located near Damascus International Airport is the
IRGC's central command and logistics center.

Northern Front: The northern front includes the
Aleppo and Idlib provinces. The command center of this
front is located at the Bahoos Garrison (situated in the
southeastern part of the al-Safireh city). The regime
has exploited religious affiliations, naming the garrison
Ruqayyah (one of the daughters of Imam Hossein, who
is buried in Syria). Following the invasion of Idlib, the
command center was moved to the industrial region of
Sheikh Najjar in northeastern Idlib. The commander
of this front is Seyyed Javad Ghaffari, who is also the
IRGC's operational commander in Syria.

Central Front: The IRGC's central front in Syria
includes the Homs, Deyr al-Zour and Raqqa provinces.
The T4 Airport near the city of Tadmar in Homs
province is one of the command and assembly centers
for the IRGC in the central front. The commander of
this front is IRGC Brigadier General Mohammad-Reza
Fallahzadeh.

Southern Front: The southern front includes parts of
the Rif, Damascus, Daraa, Qonaytareh, and al-Soveyda

provinces. The command center for IRGC forces in southern Syria is the Yarmouk University located 50 km from the Damascus to Daraa road. The IRGC has named the location Zeinab Garrison. The commander of this front is Brig. Gen. Rahim Noee Aghdam.

Coastal Front: This region includes the Tartus and Latakia. It is seen as the operations backup and logistics area for the regime's forces. The IRGC has multiple centers in this region.

Political and military intervention in Iraq

The IRGC's role in meddling in Iraqi affairs is viewed by the regime as key to the expansion of its interference in the Middle East region. Following the Iran-Iraq War in the 1980s, the Quds Force dedicated its First Corps to Iraq as the most important target for meddling. This component of the Quds Force focused on organizing Iraqi mercenaries of the IRGC known as the Badr Brigade (later known as the Badr Organization). They were previously part of the IRGC's forces. The Quds Force First Corps continued its infiltration and terrorist operations into Iraqi territory until 2003.

The invasion of Iraq by Coalition Forces in 2003 provided the regime with an excellent opportunity to expand its military presence and interference in Iraq. Following the 2003 downfall of the government in Iraq, the regional balance of power shifted in the clerical regime's favor. The withdrawal of U.S. forces from Iraq in 2009 afforded the IRGC with greater possibilities for meddling, both in political and also in military terms. Tehran increased its multi-dimensional political, military and economic meddling.

The guiding force for the regime's policies in Iraq is the Quds Force. For years, Brig. Gen. Iraj Masjedi, a veteran commander of the Quds Force, was responsible for the regime's policies in Iraq and the head of the Iraq desk at the Quds Force. All of the Iranian regime's terrorist operations in Iraq were controlled and commanded by him. In early 2017, he was appointed as the regime's ambassador to Iraq. Under the guise of its ambassador, the regime has continued meddling in Iraq.

During the May 2018 parliamentary elections in Iraq and the formation of a coalition, the clerical regime continued its extensive meddling in the elections in order to secure top posts for its agents and affiliates. Following the elections and the declaration of results, Qassem Soleimani, the Commander of the Quds Force, visited Baghdad in August 2018 in order to directly form a coalition that secures Tehran's interests. He is trying to threaten and intimidate various parties and groups to secure a larger share of power for the Iranian regime.

Warmongering in Yemen

From the time when Khamenei decided to enter into secret nuclear negotiations with the U.S., and especially after the public negotiations began in 2013, the regime prioritized meddling in regional countries and increased its efforts in this regard so that any retreat on the nuclear front would be compensated by regional gains. As such, in mid-2014, with the provocation and incitement of the Quds Force, the Yemeni civil war escalated, and the capital was overrun by Yemeni forces tied to the clerical regime in Iran. The start of the Yemeni civil war by the IRGC-affiliated Ansar Hezbollah (Houthis) forces in Yemen is considered the latest in the series of unbridled meddling in regional affairs by the IRGC.

Brig. Gen. Amirian, in charge of Arab Peninsula affairs in the Quds Force, commands IRGC-affiliated forces in Yemen. He is in constant contact with the commanders of Ansar Hezbollah.

The advance of the Ansar forces in Yemen and the threats on the border with Saudi Arabia motivated the Saudis to form a coalition of Arab countries to enter the Yemeni conflict. The Ansar forces' advance was stalled and they were forced to retreat from some Yemeni territories.

On April 14, 2015, the UN Security Council adopted a resolution with respect to the Yemeni civil war. In accordance with this resolution, any arms shipments to Ansar Hezbollah (Houthis) forces and forces tied to former President Ali Abdullah Saleh were banned. However, the IRGC continues to send missiles and a range of weaponry to Ansar Hezbollah in order to continue the conflict. Since 2015, a number of arms shipments to the Houthis from the Iranian regime have been intercepted. For instance, on January 18, 2017, a report prepared by former UN Secretary General Ban Ki-moon regarding the violation of the UN Security Council arms embargo by the Iranian regime was evaluated by the Security Council. On August 30, 2018, a boat carrying arms for the Houthis was intercepted by the U.S. Navy in the Gulf of Aden. Following an investigation, it was found that the weapons had been sent by the Iranian regime.

Interfering in Lebanon and relations with Hezbollah

In light of its Shiite minority, Lebanon has always been one of the Iranian regime's targets for the export of fundamentalism and terrorism. The clerical regime has for the past four decades extensively interfered in Lebanese affairs through the IRGC. The IRGC's direct involvement in Lebanon was made possible with the activation of its Intelligence Unit in Lebanon in 1981. However, following the creation of the Quds Force in 1990, the Quds Force's Seventh Corps, called the 7,000, was dedicated to Lebanon and Syria. In subsequent years, the IRGC command in these two countries played a logistical role for IRGC forces in other countries. For example, during the 2006 war in Lebanon, the IRGC used Syria as a logistic theater for the Lebanese war. Similarly, during the past 7 years, the IRGC has used Lebanon to support its meddling in Syria.

The extent of the Lebanese Hezbollah's dependence on the Iranian regime is so unambiguous that in a speech broadcast by the al-Manar TV station on June 26, 2017, the Secretary General of Hezbollah, Seyyed Hassan Nasrallah, declared that the Hezbollah budget, salaries, arms, and missiles are all provided by the Iranian regime.

The IRGC uses Hezbollah to manage other militias and proxies and also to conduct military and terrorist training. A report obtained from inside the regime indicates that Lebanon is the center of arms distribution and smuggling in the Middle East. Khamenei has delegated some of his designs for Arab countries to Nasrallah, giving him assignments for interference in Syria, Yemen and Bahrain. The Quds Force has transferred a portion of its command structure to Lebanon to lead its interference in Yemen. In addition, it has used the Hezbollah model to create similar militias and groups in other regional countries, sometimes even using the same name, such as the Afghan Hezbollah or the Turkish Hezbollah, among others.

The IRGC has extensively used Hezbollah for its interference in the Syrian conflict. A number of Hezbollah commanders currently reside in the Shiite city of Nabl in northwestern Aleppo, where they are responsible for commanding Syrian militia forces tied to the IRGC in Nabl and al-Zahra. The commander of this group is a Lebanese called Haj Hamzeh. The IRGC has recruited some residents of these two cities as part of its militias, and dispatched them for operations in Deyr al-Zour, Abu Kamal, and Aleppo. Their salaries are paid by the IRGC. The map below provides a picture of three Shiite-majority regions in Lebanon, which house the primary centers of the IRGC. There are also two main paths used by the IRGC and Hezbollah to move between Syria and Lebanon.

Terrorist training camps in Iran

The Quds Force, the IRGC's extraterritorial arm, has created a large directorate in order to expand its training of foreign mercenaries as part of the regime's strategy to step up its meddling abroad, including in Syria, Iraq, Yemen, Bahrain, Afghanistan and elsewhere.

Khamenei has personally expressed interest in the directorate. According to remarks by Brig. Gen. Khosrow Orouj, the former Commander of this directorate and senior advisor to the Commander-in-Chief of the IRGC,

IRGC Terrorist Training locations in Iran spread across the country and Tehran

Khamenei personally visited the Quds Force and particularly encouraged the work of this directorate.

This directorate has dozens of centers in various parts
of Iran. The training centers are organized on the basis
of the nationalities of trainees as well as the type of
training. The centers provide both terrorist training
and military training to militias to be utilized for the
regime's meddling and for advancing its objectives in
regional countries.

Hundreds are trained from Iraq, Syria, Yemen,
Afghanistan, and Lebanon in these training camps. They
are then dispatched to countries where the regime is
engaged in wars, to escalate the warmongering. Other
smaller groups are also trained for terrorist and other
operations in various countries. After 2012, the volume
of training of foreign agents in the Quds training camps
increased.

The regime also provides training for terrorist cells
for operations in countries that do not have conflicts,
including the Persian Gulf states like Bahrain and
Kuwait.

The training directorate of the Quds Force is one of
the most important sections of this terrorist force.
The directorate is codenamed 12,000 in the internal
correspondence of the IRGC. The headquarters of the
directorate is in Imam Ali Garrison located 20km from
the Tehran-Karaj Highway, Ardestani Blvd., near the
end of the Sarvan Street.[21]

---

21 See Terrorist Training Camps in Iran, published by the NCRI-US, June
   2017.

Chapter 3:
Increased Missile Threats and Violation of International Laws

One of the most important tools of the IRGC to advance the export of crises and to threaten regional countries is the creation of the IRGC missile unit and the Aerospace Organization for the mass manufacture of missiles.

The expansion of the IRGC's missiles capability is one of the three pillars of the regime's strategy after the Iran-Iraq war. These three pillars of the regime's military doctrine include the obtaining of nuclear weapons, obtaining long-range ballistic missiles, and expansion of forces for asymmetric warfare (IRGC and the Bassij).

In order to advance this military strategy, the IRGC engaged in the procurement and import of technology for the manufacturing of ballistic missiles capable of carrying a nuclear warhead.

In addition, the IRGC has used missiles as one of its most important tools for interfering in regional affairs in order to create crises and expand warmongering.

In order to expand its influence in these regions, in addition to the export of missiles to other countries in the region, the IRGC has set up missile factories in Syria, Lebanon and Iraq.

Despite the fact that the IRGC's missile activities are under sanctions through various UN Security Council resolutions, the IRGC has relied on a range of illegal procurement methods to obtain equipment and parts leveraging various international smuggling networks.[22]

Increased missile threats play a role in regional interference

During 2018, the clerical regime continued to illegally send missiles to Yemen and other regional countries in violation of UN Security Council resolutions. It has also continued terrorist operations using missiles. IRGC affiliates have used missiles made by the regime to threaten the security of regional countries. Examples include:

The Yemeni Houthis, under the command of the IRGC, continue to threaten regional countries and shipping in Bab al-Mandab with missiles. Brig. Gen. Nasser Shaabani, the Deputy Commander of Operations in Sarallah Base (in command of suppression in Tehran), said on August 7, 2018: "We told the Yemenis to target two Saudi oil tankers, and they did it. ... Hezbollah and Ansarallah are extensions of our forces. The enemy is so vulnerable that we can create conflicts for them outside our borders."[23] Several hours later, the sentence "We

---

22 Iran's Ballistic Buildup, published by the NCRI-US, May 2018.

23 Fars News Agency (IRGC-affiliated), September 7, 2018.

told the Yemenis to target two Saudi oil tankers, and they did it" was removed from the source website (both documents are attached).

According to an exclusive Reuters report, the IRGC in August 2018 sent a range of missiles to Iraq. Reuters quoted a Western source as saying: "It seems Iran has been turning Iraq into its forward missile base." The report also quoted Iranian and Iraqi sources who said a decision was made some 18 months ago to use militias to produce missiles in Iraq.[24] Reports obtained by the Iranian Resistance also indicate that the clerical regime has continually sent missiles and weaponry to militias tied to the IRGC in Iraq.

On September 8, 2018, the IRGC launched missiles against the headquarters of the Kurdish Democratic Party of Iran in Iraq. The Coordinating Center for Kurdish Parties said that as a result of the attack, 15 leaders and members of the Kurdish groups were killed and 40 others were injured. The IRGC released a statement officially claiming responsibility for the attack. Media outlets affiliated with the regime claimed that the missile attack was carried out from a launch center inside Iran. However, Bas News in Iraq's Kurdistan reported: "According to reports, the Iranian regime has created a missile launch pad in cooperation with a group from the Patriotic Union of Kurdistan. It used this launching pad located in Soleymanieh province to conduct the missile strike."[25]

---

24 Radio Farda website, August 31, 2018.

25 Bas News Agency, September 8, 2018.

Organizing the IRGC Aerospace Force and its centers

The IRGC, initially formed as ground forces, created a navy and an air force in 1985 on the orders of Khomeini. Since then, the missile unit has been embedded in the IRGC's air force. In order to expand its missile activities, it re-organized itself and in September 2009, the IRGC "Air Force" became the Aerospace Force. Since then, the commander of this force has been Brig. Gen. Amir Ali Hajizadeh. The structure of the aerospace force includes the IRGC air force, missile and anti-aircraft units. All of the regime's missiles are essentially under the control of these missile units.

The Aerospace Organization created for missile production

In order to expand missile production, the Iranian regime created an independent organization in 1996, called the Aerospace Industrial Organization (AIO) at the Defense Ministry. Currently, Brigadier General Mehrdad Akhlaqi is the commander of the AIO with a mandate of producing and proliferating ballistic missiles. In addition to the production of surface-to-surface missiles, the AIO is also involved in producing other weaponry such as surface-to-air missiles, anti-ship missiles, and surface-to-sea missiles. The two universities of Imam Hussein (tied to the IRGC) and Malek Ashtar (tied to the Defense Ministry) cooperate with the AIO in research and development. The AIO has eight independent groups for the production of various missile types, and supplies the missiles it manufactures to the missiles unit of the IRGC.

Export of weapons and missile technologies

One of the measures in line with the regime's objective of expanding warmongering in the region is creating missile factories in various countries. Relevant information includes:

The Iranian regime's former ambassador to Syria, Hossein Sheikh ol-Eslam, said in November 2016: "Since the transfer of a large quantity of missile parts and equipment cannot be done, in order to create a missile industry in territories around Iran, we have tried to make sure that this is done in those countries to the extent possible."

The commander of the IRGC Aerospace Force, Amir Ali Hajizadeh, said on November 14, 2014: "Thank God, our situation has improved today. Even the countries that helped us in those days [Iran-Iraq war], like Syria, later purchased missiles from us and now the factories for producing missiles in Syria are set up by Iran, and they produce missiles designed by Iran there."

IRGC veteran and Major General Mohammad Baqeri, the Head of the Chiefs of Staff of the regime's Armed

Aerospace Industries Organization

- Chairman's Staff
- Secretariat
- Counter-Intelligence
- Ideological – Political Office

Deputy

- Executive Directorate
- Research & Education Directorate
- Coordination Directorate
- Inspection Directorate
- Engineering Directorate
- Technical & Planning Directorate
- Export Directorate
- Financial Directorate
- Trade Directorate
- Quality Control Directorate

Ya Mahdi Missile Industries Group
- Montazer ol-Mahdi Industries
- Ansar Al-Mahdi Industries
- Shafi Zadeh Industries
- Ya Mahdi Industries Research Center

Bakeri Missiles Industries Group
- Kharrazi Industries
- Sattari Industries
- Sani Khani Industries
- Bakeri Industries Research Center

Air Defense Industries Group (Ahmad Kazemi)
- Bagheri Industries
- Babai Industries
- Sayyad Shirazi Industries
- Air Defense Industries Research Center

Cruise Industries Group (Samenol Aemme Industries)
- Fasihi Industries
- Moslemi Industries
- Rahimi Industries
- Cruise Industries Research Center

Equipment Industries Group
- Launcher and Metal Industries
- AD Guns Industries
- Tools & Machines Industries
- Mechanics Tech & Sci. Research Center

Electromechanics Industries Group (Sanam)
- Sanam Oil Industries (Shah Abadul)
- Alborz Sanam (Motahari)
- Sanam Electronics Industries
- Sanam Research Center

Fajr Industries Group (Instruments Industries)
- Fajr Industries Factory
- Fajr Research Center (Instruments)

Hemmat Missile Industrial Group
- Noori Industries
- Movahed Industries
- Varamini Industries
- Rastgar Industries
- Cheraghi Industries
- Karimi Industries
- Kalhor Industries
- Hemmat Industries Research Center

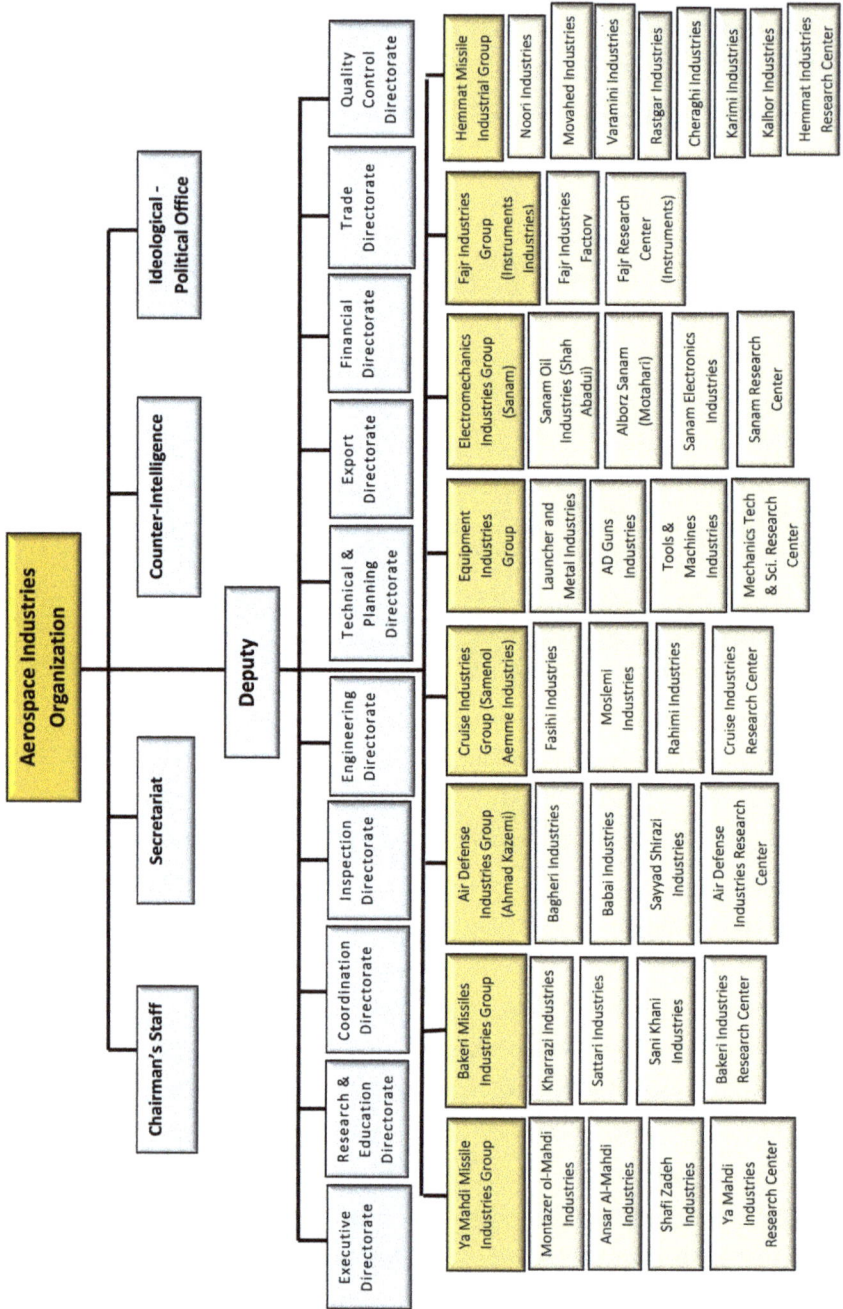

Aerospace Industries Organization Chart

IRGC Aerospace Force Flow Chart

Supreme Leader Representative

Commander of IRGC Aerospace Force B.G. Amir Ali Hajizadeh

- Clergy Affairs
- Coordinator
- Inspection & Quality Cont. Directorate
- Confirmation & Monitoring of Propaganda Office
- Engineering Unit 35

- Command & Control Center
- Security Unit
- Commander's Office
- Counter-Intelligence Unit
- Operations Directorate
- Cultural Directorate
- Human Resources Directorate
- Air Defense Directorate
- Program & Planning Directorate

- Coordination Directorate
- Counter-Intelligence

- Support
- Judicial Office
- Staff
- Investigation & Inspection Directorate
- Political Directorate
- Communications Directorate
- Medical Assistance Directorate
- Logistics Directorate
- Training Directorate

- Ammunition Command
- Maintenance Command
- Missile Unit
- Chief of Staff
- Logistics Command
- Drone Unit

Air Defense (AD) Command
- Al-Ghadir AD Missile Unit
- Ra'd AD Missile Unit

AD Groups: Meqdad 1st AD Group - Karaj; Yaser 2nd AD Group - Tehran; 3rd AD Group; Komeil 4th AD Group - Fars; Salman 5th AD Group; Abuzar 6th AD Group - Ahvaz; Hamzeh 7th AA Group - Isfahan; 8th AD Group - Kashan; 9th AD Group - Tabriz

Missile Brigades: Ghaem 16th Missile Brig.; Ra'd 5th Missile Brig.; Tohid 23rd Missile Brig.; Zolfaqar 19th Missile Brig.; Al-Hadid 7th Missile Brig.

Bases: Bushehr Base; Ahvaz Base; Martyr Karimi Airport - Kashan; Badr Base Isfahan; Ashrafi Base - Isfahan; Noshahr Base; Fath Base - Karaj; Martyr Kaveh 3rd Base; Imam Khomeini 2nd Fighter Base; Qadr 1st Mehrabad Base

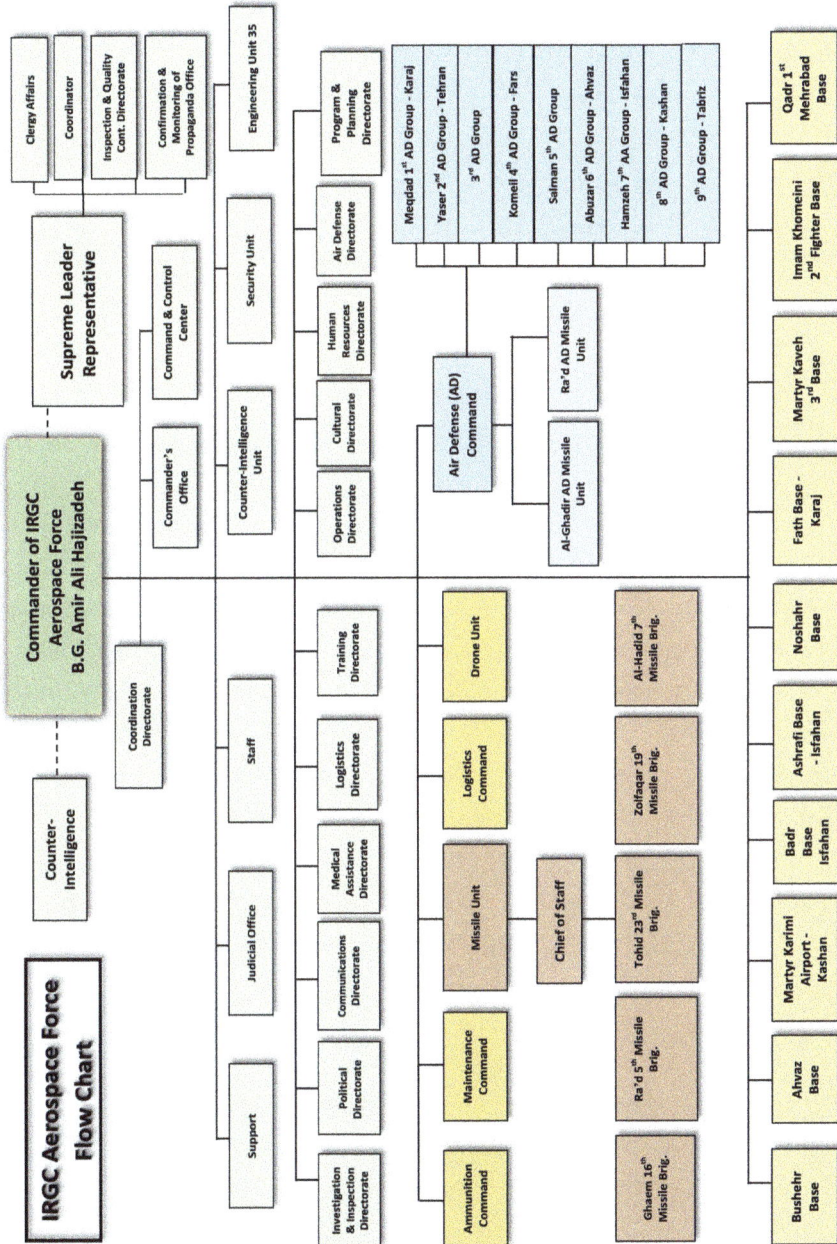

Aerospace Force Chart

Forces, said on November 10, 2016: "Syria has reached a level that has enabled Iran in recent years to set up a missile industry for it in Aleppo, where they are producing missiles." Four days later, Hajizadeh, the commander of the IRGC Aerospace, announced that the missile factories in Aleppo had been completely destroyed in the course of the conflict.

The Iranian regime's role in missile attacks in Yemen

The Houthis' ballistic missile attacks against Saudi Arabia and the United Arab Emirates in December 2017 became a matter of international importance. Presenting evidence that included parts of the launched missiles, U.S. Ambassador to the UN, Nikki Haley, declared at a press conference on December 14, 2017 that the missiles had been sent to the Houthis in Yemen by the Iranian regime. The press conference included documents indicating the Houthis used four types of weapons provided by the Iranian regime. These included the Qiam and Toufan missiles.

According to reports obtained by the Iranian Resistance from inside the IRGC, the launches of all missiles in the second half of 2017 by the Houthis in Yemen were ordered directly by the IRGC. The IRGC command told the Houthis (Ansar Hezbollah) to launch reprisal attacks against regional countries, particularly Saudi Arabia, in response to any international or regional measures against the intervention of the IRGC and its proxies

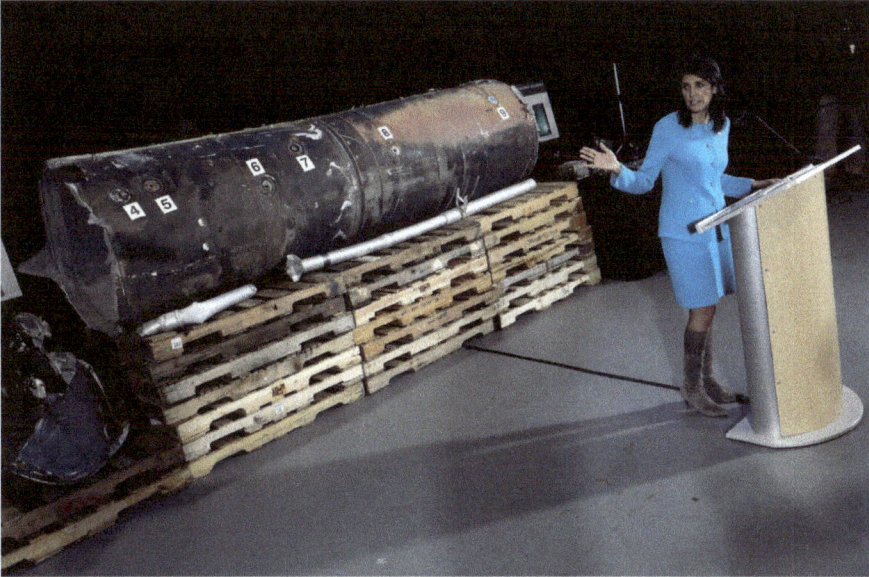

In a press conference Ambassador Nikki Haley displays missiles fired by the Iranian regime

like the Lebanese Hezbollah. According to concrete information, the missiles were made in the IRGC's Aerospace Organization factories. These reports indicate that the training to use these missiles by the Houthis was provided by IRGC experts in addition to Lebanese Hezbollah.

Conclusion

The declared and undeclared resources that the Iranian regime leverages to prolong its survival go beyond the scope of oil revenues obtained after the signing of the Joint Comprehensive Plan of Action (JCPOA) and the lifting of sanctions.

The scope of these expenditures encompasses military, armament and security budgets, domestic repression, costly state propaganda to justify suppression and terrorism, and warmongering in the rest of the Middle East, not to mention the advancement of the nuclear and missile programs.

Most of these expenditures are not openly acknowledged in the country's official budgets. Instead, the requisite funds are funneled through special accounts, the Supreme Leader Ali Khamenei's office, or the Islamic Revolutionary Guard Corps (IRGC).

The level of expenditures would be even higher if we were to consider the billions of dollars constantly embezzled and stolen by the regime's corrupt officials.

In other words, not only are oil revenues not used to improve the lot of ordinary Iranian citizens, but additionally, a large portion of other funding sources are directed toward suppression, terrorism abroad and warmongering in the region.

Furthermore, the IRGC and affiliated foundations and companies control the lion's share of the economy and trade. Half of the profits from the export and import sector end up in the coffers of the IRGC, supplying the fuel to run the extensive machinery of terror, war and plunder.

The Iranian people are experiencing these bitter realities every day with their flesh and blood. Although the mullahs are trying to blame imposition of sanctions for the appalling economic predicament, the Iranian people hold the regime and its policies accountable for their challenges, which explains why the chant of "leave Syria alone, think of us" has become a nationwide demand.

It is precisely for this reason that in the past 35 years, the Iranian Resistance has repeatedly underscored the need to impose an oil embargo against the regime, calling on the international community to prevent the regime from using the Iranian people's wealth against them and against peace and tranquility in the region.

Confronted with the real prospect of being overthrown as a result of nationwide uprisings, the mullahs' regime has panicked, and it has thus stepped up its malign activities in the region, which require even more resources and funding. In such circumstances, the international community is duty-bound to stand firm against the regime's terrorism, which threatens global peace and security, and it should refrain from paying ransom to a terrorist regime.

With the escalation of the regime's terrorist threats and behaviors, the IRGC, the Ministry of Intelligence and Security (MOIS), and affiliated organizations and companies must be treated as terrorist organizations. Moreover, all direct and indirect business dealings with them must be strictly prohibited. The regime's diplomat-terrorists and other agents must be prosecuted and face justice.

The regime's nefarious activities in the Middle East must be brought to an end and the IRGC and other regime operatives must be expelled from neighboring countries. Tehran's nuclear designs, particularly the enrichment program, must be completely dismantled.

Until and unless these objectives are met, comprehensive oil and banking sanctions must be imposed against the regime. This is an imperative for preventing the spread of terrorism, fundamentalism and warmongering in the region. Doing business with Tehran empowers and funds its pervasive machinery of terror abroad and suppression at home. Therefore, such dealings must be stopped.

List of Publications

List of Publications by the National Council of Resistance of Iran, U.S. Representative Office

Iran Will Be Free:
Speech by Maryam Rajavi

September 2018, 54 pages

This manuscript contains delivered keynote speech by Mrs. Maryam Rajavi, on June 30, 2018, at the Iranian Resistance's grand gathering in Paris, France explaining the path to freedom in Iran and what she envisions for future Iran.

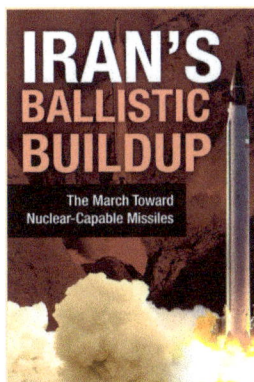

Iran's Ballistic Buildup: The March Toward Nuclear-Capable Missiles

May 2018, 136 pages

This manuscript surveys Iran's missile capabilities, including the underlying organization, structure, production, and development infrastructure, as well as launch facilities and the command centers. The book exposes the nexus between the regime's missile activities and its nuclear weapons program, including ties with North Korea.

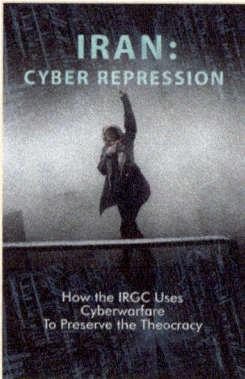

Iran: Cyber Repression: How the IRGC Uses Cyberwarfare to Preserve the Theocracy
February 2018, 70 pages

This manuscript demonstrates how the Iranian regime, under the supervision and guidance of the IRGC and the Ministry of Intelligence and Security (MOIS), have employed new cyberwarfare and tactics in a desperate attempt to counter the growing dissent inside the country.

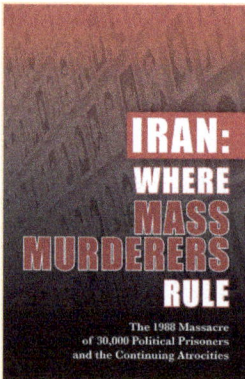

Iran: Where Mass Murderers Rule: The 1988 Massacre of 30,000 Political Prisoners and the Continuing Atrocities
November 2017, 161 pages

Iran: Where Mass Murderers Rule is an expose of the current rulers of Iran and their track record in human rights violations. The book details how 30,000 political prisoners fell victim to politicide during the summer of 1988 and showcases the egregious political extinction of a group of people.

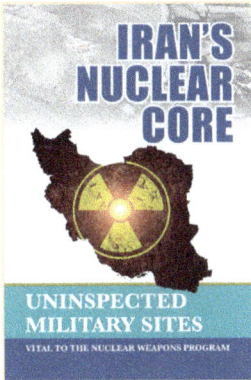

Iran's Nuclear Core: Uninspected Military Sites, Vital to the Nuclear Weapons Program

October 2017, 52 pages

This book details how the nuclear weapons program is at the heart of, and not parallel to, the civil nuclear program of Iran. The program has been run by the Islamic Revolutionary Guards Corp (IRGC) since the beginning, and the main nuclear sites and nuclear research facilities have been hidden from the eyes of the United Nations nuclear watchdog.

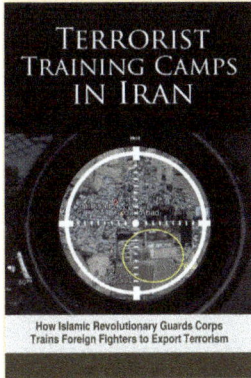

Terrorist Training Camps in Iran: How Islamic Revolutionary Guards Corps Trains Foreign Fighters to Export Terrorism

June 1017, 56 pages

The book details how Islamic Revolutionary Guards Corps trains foreign fighters in 15 various camps in Iran to export terrorism. The IRGC has created a large directorate within its extraterritorial arm, the Quds Force, in order to expand its training of foreign mercenaries as part of the strategy to step up its meddling abroad in Syria, Iraq, Yemen, Bahrain, Afghanistan and elsewhere.

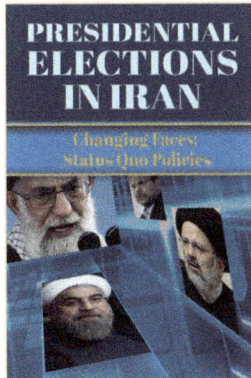

Presidential Elections in Iran: Changing Faces; Status Quo Policies

May 2017, 78 pages

The book reviews the past 11 presidential elections, demonstrating that the only criterion for qualifying as a candidate is practical and heartfelt allegiance to the Supreme Leader. An unelected vetting watchdog, the Guardian Council makes that determination.

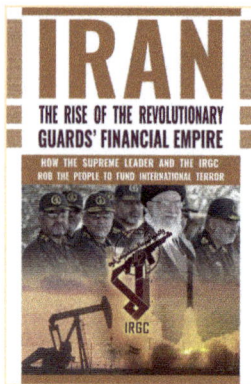

The Rise of Iran's Revolutionary Guards' Financial Empire: How the Supreme Leader and the IRGC Rob the People to Fund International Terror

March 2017, 174 pages

This manuscript examines some vital factors and trends, including the overwhelming and accelerating influence (especially since 2005) of the Supreme Leader and the Islamic Revolutionary Guard Corps (IRGC). This study shows how ownership of property in various spheres of the economy is gradually shifted from the population writ large towards a minority ruling elite comprised of the Supreme Leader's office and the IRGC, using 14 powerhouses, and how the money ends up funding terrorism worldwide.

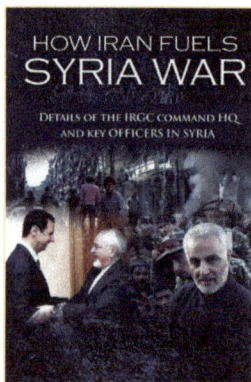

How Iran Fuels Syria War: Details of the IRGC Command HQ and Key Officers in Syria

November 2016, 74 pages

This book examines how the Iranian regime has effectively engaged in the military occupation of Syria by marshaling 70,000 forces, including the Islamic Revolutionary Guard Corps (IRGC) and mercenaries from other countries into Syria; is paying monthly salaries to over 250,000 militias and agents to prolong the conflict; and divided the country into 5 zones of conflict, establishing 18 command, logistics and operations centers.

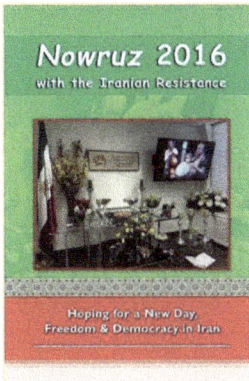

Nowruz 2016 with the Iranian Resistance: Hoping for a New Day, Freedom and Democracy in Iran

April 2016, 36 pages

This book describes Iranian New Year, Nowruz celebrations at the Washington office of Iran's parliament-in-exile, the National Council of Resistance of Iran. The yearly event marks the beginning of spring. It includes select speeches by dignitaries who have attended the NCRIUS Nowruz celebrations. This book also discusses the very rich culture and the traditions associated with Nowruz for centuries.

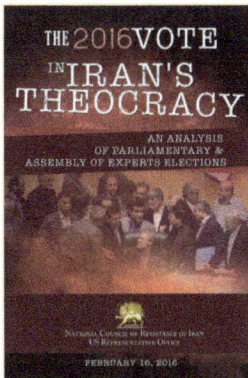

The 2016 Vote in Iran's Theocracy: An analysis of Parliamentary & Assembly of Experts Elections

February 2016, 70 pages

This book examines all the relevant data about the 2016 Assembly of Experts as well as Parliamentary elections ahead of the February 2016 elections. It looks at the history of elections since the revolution in 1979 and highlights the current intensified infighting among the various factions of the Iranian regime.

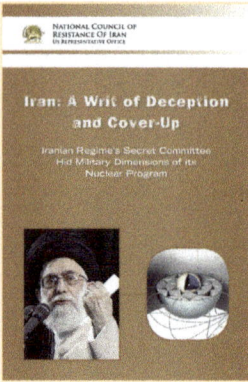

IRAN: A Writ of Deception and Cover-up: Iranian Regime's Secret Committee Hid Military Dimensions of its Nuclear Program
February 2016, 30 pages

The book provides details about a top-secret committee in charge of forging the answers to the International Atomic Energy Agency (IAEA) regarding the Possible Military Dimensions (PMD) of Tehran's nuclear program, including those related to the explosive detonators called EBW (Exploding Bridge Wire) detonator, which is an integral part of a program to develop an implosion type nuclear device.

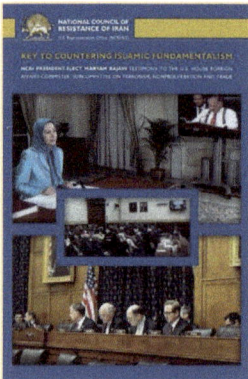

Key to Countering Islamic Fundamentalism: Maryam Rajavi? Testimony To The U.S. House Foreign Affairs Committee
June 2015, 68 pages

Testimony before U.S. House Foreign Affairs Committee's subcommittee on Terrorism, non-Proliferation, and Trade discussing ISIS and Islamic fundamentalism. The book contains Maryam Rajavi's full testimony as well as the question and answer by representatives.

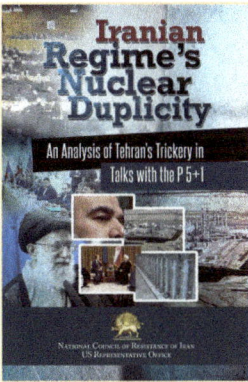

Iranian Regime's Nuclear Duplicity:
An Analysis of Tehran's Trickery in Talks with the P 5+1

January 2016, 74 pages

This book examines Iran's behavior throughout the negotiations process in an effort to inform the current dialogue on a potential agreement. Drawing on both publicly available sources and those within Iran, the book focuses on two major periods of intense negotiations with the regime: 2003-2004 and 2013-2015. Based on this evidence, it then extracts the principles and motivations behind Tehran's approach to negotiations as well as the tactics used to trick its counterparts and reach its objectives.

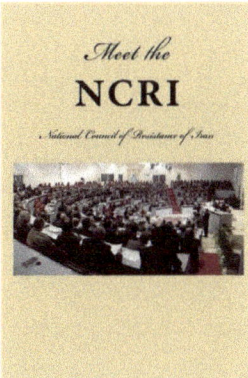

Meet the National Council of Resistance of Iran

June 2014, 150 pages

Meet the National Council of Resistance of Iran discusses what NCRI stands for, what its platform is, and why a vision for a free, democratic, secular, non-nuclear republic in Iran would serve world peace.

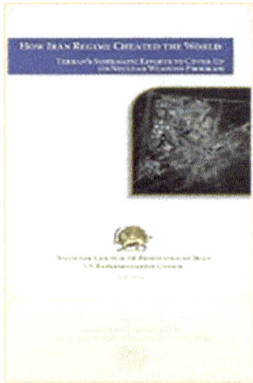

How Iran Regime Cheated the World: Tehran's Systematic Efforts to Cover Up its Nuclear Weapons Program

June 2014, 50 pages

This book deals with one of the most fundamental challenges that goes to the heart of the dispute regarding the Iranian regime's controversial nuclear program: to ascertain with certainty that Tehran will not pursue a nuclear bomb. Such an assurance can only be obtained through specific steps taken by Tehran in response to the international community's concerns. The monograph discusses the Iranian regime's report card as far as it relates to being transparent when addressing the international community's concerns about the true nature and the ultimate purpose of its nuclear program

About the NCRI-US

The National Council of Resistance of Iran-US Representative Office acts as the Washington office for Iran's parliament-in-exile, which is dedicated to the establishment of a democratic, secular, non-nuclear republic in Iran.

NCRI-US, registered as a non-profit tax-exempt organization, has been instrumental in exposing the nuclear weapons program of Iran, including the sites in Natanz, and Arak, the biological and chemical weapons program of Iran, as well as its ambitious ballistic missile program.

NCRI-US has also exposed the terrorist network of the Iranian regime, including its involvement in the bombing of Khobar Towers in Saudi Arabia, the Jewish Community Center in Argentina, its fueling of sectarian violence in Iraq and Syria, and its malign activities in other parts of the Middle East.

Our office has provided information on the human rights violations in Iran, extensive anti-government demonstrations, and the movement for democratic change in Iran.

Visit our website at www.ncrius.org

You may follow us on   twitter🐦 @ncrius

Follow us on   f facebook. NCRIUS

You can also find us on   NCRIUS
                                    📷 Instagram

www.ingramcontent.com/pod-product-compliance
Lightning Source LLC
Chambersburg PA
CBHW051249020426
42333CB00025B/3124